The Rules of Love and War

Shel Shamus

Table of Contents

The Marriage in the Divorce

The Re-Marriage

4

The Dance

We live in a world of power. Whether it's in the home or in the world. Wars are normal. So are fights. We want to love. But we fear. So we protect and fight. Even each other. Cat fights and long nights.

It's a dance. We don't want to give up our position too easily. We don't want to lose. We want to come together. We want to be happy. But there are all these rules that we don't even know we are abiding by.

You can do this. But you can't do that. But you can later. In certain confines. You can do this now. But not now.

We all want the same thing. But part of us is afraid. Which part wins? Only one. Or we end up unhappy when we "win." And happy when we don't fight.

But it is ourselves we are fighting. But we all know it's the other person. Or our parents. Or society—the way things are. Or the law—I can use that to co-sign my bullshit. And that knowledge is the problem.

So we dance. We try to be free. But our fear dictates otherwise. And we all agree. So it's hard. You can't fuck him. Or else. You can't fight her. Or else.

You can't compromise in the middle east. We can't let them do that. We make sure we think that all the time. Without knowing it. Just watch the news any day. Though some do know it. Some try and dissent. Some to orgasms. Some to jail. And some know exactly what they are doing. And they may control all of us. On a micro level or in the world. Though we don't know them. And we don't know we imitate them. It's extreme unflattey. But we all do it. And are shunned for not. It's a self-fulfilling prophecy.

Why are Nelson Mandela and Ghandi our heroes?
We would never know. Because we are too afraid
to do what they do. We can be satisfied with our
next piece of cheese. Whatever trickles down.
Though most of us will never question this stuff.
How we fall victim to it; perpetuate it; create it.
When they say we killed the Kennedys, it's not just
a song. Our reward may have been the Beatles. But
we don't hear them either. Not now john we will
never understand. Nor the point of Hollywood
tragedies—as opposed to Hollywood endings. Or
the point of Hollywood at all. It's more than
popcorn.

And the radio. So many heroes. So many prophets.
We revere Bob Dylan and Johnny Cash. But can we
hear Jimmy?

No. We are too afraid of losing what we have. Or
not getting what we want. Even if it's just our pride.
It is framed as security. Protecting our children.

Protecting women. But from who? It really is the media. It really is our belief system. And it is very easy to meet the threat if it really exists. Pepper spray. And live free. Very few are in any real danger. Though you would never know it from the news we feed off of every night. Unless it is from those who are protecting us. Like computer virus companies creating the viruses that they protect us from.

So we dance. We all want to fuck. We all want love. We all want success. But we feel like we have to do a number of dances first. Or we can't do it. Even worse. And we don't even know it. And we are shunned if we do.

So we spend our youth on our old age. And our old age on our youth. And we have to reach for hopes or memories to justify both. Instead of really living the dream. If you ask anyone in their golden years, they will tell you everything what they did wrong. But can't do any more. That's why they act exactly as they want. They know there is nothing to fear anymore. And that they owe their lives to no one. But we know better.

As this dance is magnified in our world. This country did this to us. This country did that to us. Or there is oil. Or poppy seeds. But we need to believe in the threat. So we dance.

Fear! Anger! Hurt another. Feel better. Dance! As it is really us that shoots ourselves in the feet, so to speak.

We don't even see the invisible rules. The invisible scaffolding of this world. Some of it comes from inside. Some of it out. And it recreates itself through us. Because it couldn't without. In our small lives. And in the bigger world. But it's all the same. Like a fractal. Everything we do matters. Every single action. It co-creates the world every day.

Our fears rule us. Our anger from it relieves us. They are the law. Those are the rules. It starts with our families. And we do the same. And if we grow up to be president. Nothing is different. A child is in office. She has just been taught another series of niceties and appropriateness—which she dare not stray from—that makes her look like an adult.

We are still children. We just have more hair. Some of us get to live in our terrible twos—finally free. Others have to be good. Others don't. the ones at the top, or dressed as a cop, don't either.

Shame works well. Fear works well. Removing security to take it back seems to work perfectly. Or at least pretending. So you can take.

Though we offer up our liberty. And our security. Without knowing how secure and free we already were. We buy something that is already ours. And sell it to buy it. And so on.

The Sex

When our pride is satisfied, either out or inside, we finally come full circle. We finally come around. He started it. So it's okay. Or not. We come either way. One may be much better. But the other may be our release. From the conflicts in our mind. Unless we make them in our real lives. If we need to justify.

But we come. Usually everybody finds the exit sign from the maze. Marriage. Or war. It makes it okay. My preacher said so. Though I haven't respected him for years. Or relationship will do. Even though I want all these other guys. How do I reconcile. I get approval from my tribe. I get approval from my pride. It never occurred to me that I could just look inside. Or at my own body and find. All that I am looking for outside. It's a free ride. But we charge—and charge ourselves—and all agree on the price.

It's not just women. It's not just men. It's something bigger. Even if we're bigger than that.

Women do their part. And men theirs. Whether its no sex and instead a purse made in Italy—or deferring to the man and a car made in Germany. When we come, we do so appropriately. Until we mate marry and fuck. In some form.

Even the liberals failed us. They say the same thing. They are just new preachers in Nietzsche's garb. God may be dead, but he lives on through us. Never mind that Nietzsche told us we could be better. That we all could overcome. It's really a funny story. Sex killed him.

But sex is okay. If you do it this way. So long as you buy what we want you to buy on your way there. And we don't know any better. We all worship the ring. The dollar. The shiny things. All they have to do is incite our pride. There is one path you can take. Monogamy. Monandry. And buy all the way up. A house. Two cars. Jewelry. Christmas changed from love to consumerism. It could be Christmas every day. We are the gift. And the recipient. Instead we're Molassses. Waiting for Godot. Who really does sit atop us on a throne. An old man or woman with silver hair. Or a group of them. They decide interest rates. And fiscal policy. And sexual behavior. And make it worth everybody's while. One way or another. Those that say this end up dead. If they are heard. But they can only kill one at a time. For now. To scare the rest of us. That might agree or disagree. They decide the rules. But have to impregnate our minds with them for a lifetime. They know we are our own kings and queens. But we don't. So they hunt a herd of cattle for now.

The Commitment

So we commit. Whether we realize it or not. To the ways of the world. To the marriage with it. And if we do what we are supposed to do, we get to get marred and have love. We get to have a house and two cars. We get to have children. We get respect. And that allows all of it.

Once we've followed all the rules, we get to get love from others. As if we didn't already have it from ourselves. It's a paradox. Everybody needs each other's approval—is each other's judge. But few, if anybody are solid inside. We're all wind vanes. It's a house of cards. For each of us. And all of us. Where does the wind come from? Each other? Or somewhere else.

But if we commit to the just the way things are, we're okay. We are a face planet. It all depends on how we look. We are all empty inside waiting for

that laugh or nod. But they need it from you too.
But where does the wind come from? It's just each
other. Our "friends." Our family. Our society. Or
somewhere else. That we don't know we're
cosigning. TV? Movies? Music? The news? I don't
know. Listen and find out.

So we "commit" to each other. It keeps us safe. In
the lines. Off the radar—if we can see that far. And
allows us to come. Comeittment.

Maybe we need to be committed... But we commit
those who say otherwise. In one way or another.
We've been hacked. So we agree. We bow. We are
okay. Because someone else says so. Until we
become the king and queen in a new way. Then
that status, that face, is the sex we need.

The Marriage

So you I do thee wed. Says someone else to us. As if we have to ask them. It's been this way for so long, we don't know the difference. And we love the ceremony. The achievement. Our lives are one repeated series of the exact same events. The big scores in life. Coming of age. Marriage. Death. And taxes. All bequeathed by a Preacher of some kind. Or a government. Or our frineds. Or our family. As if we needed their approval. It's all one big hierarchy.

We are to be separate until we are approvable. A constant battle to make sure. I will be funnier. I will be cooler. I will be dominant. I will keep my power. I will step on you. Or if you do it my way, you will be okay. Fall in line. Then you get what you deserve.

The same thing happens in politics. The congress or President have to do what they are told too. Or else they go to jail, lose their lives, or die. Die. Unless…. You want to move up in the world… You do don't you? But once you marry the mafia, it's well known in Catholicism: you can't get a divorce.

The marriage is we agree. Because we are too afraid. Or we don't know any better. Then you can get married. And have sex. And have money. And be funny. We actually decide. But we are too inundated with "the truth." And never know it for real. That no one owns us. No one owns our body. No one owns our decisions. But what about the Joneses? What will they think? Even though we don't even know them.

The Honeymoon

Then we get to enjoy the fruits of compliance. Cars, women, men, status, nice houses, paid vacations, etc. We know we are right at this point. It is obvious. All is well. We have everything we want. Or are on our way to it. We are living the American dream. Everyone wants a piece. It doesn't matter what we have to give up to get it. Our ethics, our dreams of freedom or equality from college, another person; and, eventually, our rights, our freedom, and our safety, which we think we are earning.

We are living it up. We go to bars and drink away any confusion. We go to movies and miss the point. We sit in the backyard with friends and drink. It's high school but with a craftsman or Tudor façade.

And we get to fuck whenever we want! That's the clincher. No more awkward nights at the bar or coffee shop trying to get laid. No more rosy palm as our best friend. We are totally free. As long as its okay with our wife.

We are living the dream. Or in a dream world. Either way. All we have to do is look at the huge flat screen. Or the size of our house. Or the size of the SUV. And the brand. And at our wife. All we have to do is look around us and know that everything is okay inside. Instead of ever having to look inside. We can live our whole lives and never have to think. Except numbers. Or problem solving. Or bank accounts. Or the corporate ladder. Prostrate to another at work. Maybe at home too. Middle management is endless. Each new title a reward. Each 2.5% raise a reward. Each coo from the higher middle management a reward.

We love it. We drank all the way through college for this. I would say the white picket fence. But its too cliché' at this point. The fence is our collar. It is embedded in our spine at this point. Maybe someday partner in the good we're doing for our clients in our industry. Or a fatter paycheck. Either way.

Money is our shining star. It gives us the greatest orgasm. And allows all other orgasms. All is well. Just keep calm and stay busy. It worked for the middle and lower classes all these years. We are now safe finally. And as long as we do things within the lines, we will stay safe.

The Plateau and Appeasement

Now we have to keep it. At any cost. Protect our wives. Protect our children. Protect our bank accounts. So we now have to stay between the lines. So ethical sacrifices seem far away at this point. We now have something to lose. Something that can be taken away. So we just do as we're told. By our bosses. By the government. By our spouse. And don't know what we are giving up by doing so.

We have to keep this high forever. We have to work to pay the mortgage. To pay the lease on our car to get to work. To pay the mortgage. And the lease on our car.

We are locked in. But the fleshpots, the benefits, the comfort, keeps us on time. Like Pavlov's dogs. We have reached the plateau. We will never admit to ourselves, or our spouses, or our friends, that we may not be happy. If this is not it, what is?

So we stay in the trenches. And save for our childhood. Old age. When we can't fuck anymore. And we can barely move. At which point many of us realize what really matters. We know we can hit on anyone. We know we don't have to people please. Hierarchies don't mean a thing. We know we don't have to take shit from anyone. But it's too late. And, for others, and even some of the former, luckily, alcohol is still there.

So we end up in appeasement. A form of extortion. And the only way to keep oneself is not to appease or be extorted. One can't give one's power away. Appeasement is the first step towards being a hostage. That lesson was learned in World War II when the allies wanted t keep the peace so badly they gave in to everything the Nazis did to avoid war. It did not succeed but there were huge losses from it.

The Back and Forth

At this point, we know we still have most or all of the pain we always had. The façade is pretty. Our spouse may be pretty. Our clothes may be pretty. But we are turning inside. Half our marriages end. The speed limit prevents our midlife sports car purchase from doing much good. We are finally free from our kids. But this is the way it is. We are still unhappy. And whatever heroine we choose still doesn't work. After three days we are just chasing the dragon—our tail. We can't tell anyone. Nor can they tell us. Nor can we admit we see a therapist. Or take pills. We are the same as when we started. The mask of work may work at times. Or looking around us at all the pretty expensive things and people may distract us for a moment. But we go to sleep alone. Even if we're not on the couch. And we wake up alone. Along with all those other moments during the day we can't distract with status or money or husbands or wives. When we awake, we quickly feel for our spouse. When we dress for work we look at how adult we are. When we are at work we are calm because we are busy in the spinning wheel. No matter who it's producing energy for. We spend all our time "getting out of ourselves." Because we really are just as unhappy as we've always been. TV helps. Movies and Music. But never are we okay.

So we fight again. Our wives and husbands and partners! Our friends unless we get the drinking on early. Our co-workers me might keep a low profile to keep our power. And inside the war rages. It's the back and forth. Inside, manifest outside. But we don't know that's the source of all our problems. And the place to fix them. It has to be the other person. Or the boss. Or the co-worker. Or the spouse. Another new car? A new TV? Another future ex-spouse? Siri?

So we fight. We watch others fight. We watch countries fight. And love it. Even if it hurts.

Especially if it hurts. That's what makes it so tasty. We manifest a world of war. All the way from the source. Not North Korea. Us. Inside us. To North Korea. North Korea??? But there is this reason and that reason. This exception and that justification. It keeps our inner hamster wheel spinning. And we keep calm and stay busy. We may vote to nuke somebody. But we feel better.

So the back and forth, be it inside, becomes outside. Our own struggles become the world's struggles. Some people want this. But they stay invisible. But we agree. And that makes it work. How do we agree? We don't know any better. We believe our nipple, be it poison or not. The news, some TV and Movies. Video games to train our children. Competition excites us. But instead of keeping it in the stadium, which is dubious in itself, as it distracts us from something better. Something inside, we create a stadium of our life—and the world. And it is real lives that are at stake. We might say "so long as its not ours." But it really is. And always has been. Just open any history book. We don't see beyond the present. Or even that. We don't see beyond our nose.

The Makeup Sex

So after the fight, we fuck. And all is well. Be that our spouse, friends, peace in the middle east, or a drink after our team loses. Or a raise or a promotion or a new suit. Whatever we might have a problem with goes away—like magic. The problem is created—and the answer appears. From our little lives—to the world. But we don't see beyond the veil. The virus that is created so they can solve it. We are all fish. We all bite. We are all caught. And we never see it. And if we do, God help us. We can't stray from the norm. The pack. Where we are safe.

So we fuck and get it all out. Or call it something else. We get paid for it. It's been the same profession since we can remember. Only we thought it was "those other people." Because we do it like everybody else. So it's okay. As we take our toke. Or cut off an old lady in traffic. Or profit off the back end. Or "lose" that evidence from the arrest: no one will miss an ounce here or there.

An orgasm does take away our mind. As does a beer. As does the hamster wheel. That is us making up with ourselves, proxied by unseen forces. You will fight; you will love it; then you will feel better. We promise.

The Afterglow or the Divorce

So we kill our mind, we feel better, and we go with that. We ignore the problems. We ignore our inner suffering. We look again at our spouse, or job, or car—and keep telling ourselves its okay. Not the most beautiful afterglow. But its all most of us have.

Or we win by fighting; we divorce, we quit; we demand a raise; we find our strength, then are divorced. We won, so that is the afterglow. It's usually either deference or competition. Rarely cooperation. That's what's modeled. That's what we do. Or we can't wait to see that bomb go down that air vent.

It makes us happy, though it is just a crack hit. It doesn't last very long. And we won't be okay without another. But we don't know another option. Or if we do, we usually keep it to ourselves.

Because it's cooler.   Even at 50. We don't really want to rock the boat do we?

So we stay in the center of the boat. We do what others do. We don't want to differ. We don't want to lose respect. We don't want to be the outcast. So everyone tells everyone else its okay. In one way or another. Even though we're all just mirrors for each other. It's a paradox. It's unstable. It's fake. It's painful. But all we have to do is look over at our friend—and, if they smile, it's okay.

So, again, we all agree. Because we are all scared. But we feel better. Until we need that next smile or joke or beer. Crack is a funny thing.

The Marriage in the Divorce

So we may split up. We may let drama loose us friends or family. We may move to the other side of the house. But we can't divorce from the life. And worse, we can't divorce from our worst saboteur, our own mind. The root of all of this.

So we are married to the mafia. But we are it. We will never give up those smiles or jokes. We give them to each other. Also because we are scared. But if we never say it, it isn't true. It's like a reflection of a reflection of a reflection of the light. It makes no sense. But we have been living in it since grade school. And we know no better. The alimony never stops. The protection never stops. And the child support never stops—which is really for us. We are the children.

Even in divorce there is marriage. Even the rebel isn't different or special without the institution. So we stay married—in one way or another: to the people, places, and things around us. To the institutions. Etc.

The root of it is our unseen marriage to our thoughts and feelings, which we don't know aren't us. Thus we are kneeling to them—and whatever god they lead us to. Anything from heroin to chocolate.. From money to status. From beauty to codependency. From orgasm to power trip.

And these "little" trips build the planetary reality. We are the world. Or our corner of it. We are either part of the problem or part of the solution. There really is no abstinence. But abstinence is better than antagonist. Can we divorce from this mess? Can we really remarry?

The Re-Marriage

Yes we can! We can divorce ourselves from our inner demons; our emotions and thoughts, like any Buddhist. The more of us who do this the better the planet becomes—heals. If we overcome ourselves first, then we can overcome everything, including the system; or "the man."

Overcoming ourselves mean awareness of self, separation from it: because lower forces can control us without our knowledge. Some call it having a good wolf and a bad wolf inside us. And the one we feed is the one we become. Some call it a form of "dying" to oneself. Giving up all our baggage, causes, resentments, seven deadly sins, etc. Some call it medittion. It takes work—and a while. But then we can truly be divorces from the invisible rules of love and war that we now follow— massacre—and remarry much happier and more successfully: to work, play spouses, causes, etc....

We can remarry. Mainly a selfless and cleansed self. A self that does not have to win. A self that needs not, but can indulge with the power of choice and moderation. A self that doesn't seek to hurt or run from the truth of hurting others. A self that knows there are two paths you can go on, no pun intended: love or non-involvement: both inside and out.

Those are the real rules of love and war: love or non-involvement. And don't give yourself away. No one owns you or can control you. Even with a gun to your head. You can survive and thrive in any situation. There can be a myriad of corollaries to these three rules. But that's basically it—for the planet and each of us.

Until then, in self-defense one can fight. But with honor and respect. We don't involve innocents. We honor our foe, dead or alive. We respect each other. We treat each other as we would want to be treated if one needs to simplify the complexities of honor and respect. We are each other too. Even our foe. We all have the same spirit. And your foe could be your father next time. Your rapist could be your mother. Your abuser could be your son or daughter.

What's more, its us that suffer the most over lack of respect, honor compassion, forgiveness, only fighting in self-defense, fighting with care—as minimally as possible.

We can point out specifically compassion, forgiveness, honor, respect, no gossiping, no civilian or innocent casualties, no unwarranted attacks. Not committing "the seven deadly sins", for the most part. And if we choose love over fear, we will impact the planet. The bigger version of our cat fights. The bigger part of the fractal.

The universe is a big place with a lot of complicated truths. And the more we simplify, the better off we are. The more we choose love, the more we save ourselves. And it ripples to and through others.

The re-marriage is, first, with ourselves. Then we are whole and need no others. Then every marriage—with ever person, place, thing, or institution is in love. As are we.